How to Analyze People with Psychology

The Ultimate Guide to Speed Reading People through Body Language Analysis and Behavior Psychology

Emotional Pathway

Table of Contents

IN THE MIDDLE

Thoughts and Lessons Learned
from an Olympic Medalist

Terin Humphrey

ISBN: 9781692280550

The author disclaims responsibility for adverse effects or consequences from the misapplication or injudicious use of the information contained in this book. Mention of resources and associations does not imply an endorsement.

Cover photo by Juliet Photography
http://julietimage.weebly.com

Dedication

There are so many individuals who have come in my life and have left an impression. I would like to dedicate this book to my family. My family gave me the courage to tell my story and share it with all of you. My hope is that everyone reading this book knows they have a purpose in life and to cherish every moment they have.

Table of Contents

Introduction

First, let me introduce myself. My name is Terin Humphrey. I'm a small-town country girl who is the most stubborn, hard-headed, hardest worker out there. When I competed in gymnastics and my coach would tell me to do 10 of something, I made sure I did 12. I have always driven for perfection. I want to be better each day.

I came from a very hard-working family. My dad was the vice president of a bank, cleaned the bank and gym a few nights a week, and built houses on nights and weekends to pay for my gymnastics. My mom worked at a flower shop and cleaned the bank and gym at nights. She ran me to and from practice every day. Now she works in real estate, and she is my biggest fan.

When I decided to pursue my dreams to train at the best gym in Missouri, Great American Gymnastics Express, it meant my brother had to switch schools. That was a big sacrifice he made, and it's one that I will always appreciate. He joined the Marines right after the devastating events of 9/11 and served a tour in Iraq. Later he became a Sergeant for the Blue Springs

Police Department and led the SWAT Team. He is currently pursuing his dream of becoming a lawyer and has two sons and a daughter.

By now you might be wondering why the book is titled *In the Middle*. The reason is because my entire life, I have been in the middle of everything. As a police officer, I was forced to be a "good guy," but I also had to relate to the "bad guys." As an ex-athlete on the Selection Committee, I was forced to make decisions based solely on what was best for the country's needs while at the same time empathizing with the athletes since I understood what they were going through. And in life, I constantly find myself in situations where I am in the middle.

I've been asked, "Why now, Terin? Why come out with a book now?" The answer is because I want to tell my story. I want people to know that I've always done my best with every situation that I have encountered. I am an Olympic athlete, and no one can take that away, but at the same time, I have experienced so much more. As you start this book, I want to be clear: this is not a story about my Olympic journey. Although the Olympics were a huge part of my life, they were not my whole life. In these pages, I want to share even more with you. As a competitor, a female athlete, and in my professional career, I have experienced so much. My hope is that in my story you will find something that speaks to you, and that perhaps something here will help you if you are stuck "in the middle."

Chapter 1

School

I first moved to the Kansas City area from a small town called Albany, Missouri. At first, my family drove me an hour and a half twice a week for private lessons. My coach told my parents that if I wanted a college scholarship or wanted to take my gymnastics career even further, I would have to move to Kansas City so I could come to the gym on a consistent basis. As crazy as it might sound to some people, we made the decision to do that. My mom and I moved into a small apartment for a year by ourselves to see if I enjoyed training with Al Fong and Armine Barutyan-Fong. This move was very scary. Moving to the big city of Kansas City was a huge change from the small town where I grew up. It was also really tough living without my dad and brother. Despite those challenges, we made it work.

After a year on our own, my brother and dad moved down and joined us. For obvious reasons, my brother was very hesitant about this move. He was not happy about moving away from his school friends. I felt bad that my entire family made such a huge sacrifice for me. This gave me even more incentive to do my best.

I ended up training over 40 hours a week. At first, I trained before and after school. However, it was really hard for all the athletes to juggle both. We were constantly late to school, so I ended up going to school from 7:30 a.m. to noon and trained from 1:00 p.m. to 7:00 p.m. I was able to count my gymnastics as a PE credit and did a couple of online classes, but it was still really challenging. By seventh and eighth grade, my parents decided it was just easier to homeschool.

In homeschool, I started my day by getting up at the same time my brother got up for school. I had workbooks to do, and when I needed help, my mom or dad taught me. There were some fun parts about homeschooling. One thing I really enjoyed was when my mom and I would go outside in the mornings and do different creative outdoor activities. At the same time, I missed my friends, and I begged my family to put me back in a normal high school. I needed an outlet besides going back and forth to the gym and home every day.

Based on my experience, I would say it is very important for kids to be able to go to a normal public school or a school that is someplace other than home. It allows athletes to interact with "normal" people who are not involved in gymnastics. I enjoyed hanging out with my classmates because when I had a bad day in the gym, my school classmates did not care. They never asked about my gymnastics or asked questions about why I couldn't do a certain skill because they did not understand gymnastics. They liked me as a person and not as the gymnast.

Having said that, I have to admit that I was a very shy kid. I kept to myself for the most part but did have two girlfriends. We used to attend football games every Friday night. It was hard to manage both school and gymnastics. However, I made it work. Often times I would get to school early enough to receive help from my teachers with homework if I needed it. I did homework in the car and any free moment I had. When I was out competing and representing the USA, I would ask my teachers if I could receive my homework ahead of time so I would not run so far behind.

Organization was key to my success. I made the commitment to go back to high school, so I had to make it work. There were some days that I would be away from home for weeks at a time. I give credit to my teachers. They were so patient with me and helped me every step of the way. I always say, to make an Olympic team there has to be an entire package – the athlete, the parents, the teachers, the teammates, the attitude, and hard work. If something is missing from that equation, it will be more difficult.

The summer before my freshman year of high school, my coach went in to the school and encouraged them to support my Olympic dream. My school was very supportive and allowed me the flexibility I needed. I attended Odessa High School and graduated in May of 2004. That summer, in August 2004, I attended the Olympics in Athens, Greece.

Action Box:

Who is in your support system?

Write down three things that help you stay on track with your daily schedule.

- *Example: I write lists of my daily, weekly, monthly, and yearly tasks.*

1. ....

   ....

   ....

2. ....

   ....

   ....

3. ....

   ....

   ....

   ....

Chapter 2

No Regrets

I trained 40+ hours a week. In the summertime, the elite athletes trained two times a day. We went in from 8:00 a.m. to noon or 1:00 p.m. and went back around from 3:00 p.m. to 6:00 or 6:30 p.m. My dad put in a pool so during our breaks we caught up on some Vitamin D and rested our legs in the cool water. My teammates and I switched houses to rest at during our break so our parents could work a normal work schedule.

Our training consisted of bars and beam every day, twice a day, and we rotated leg events (vault and floor) every other day. There were some days we would be on bars up to three hours a day! I had no complaints because I loved bars, and it was my favorite event. I could do any skill my coach had me do on the uneven bars. It came easily and naturally for me. When I was on them, I felt like a kid on the jungle gym! I felt bad for the girls who got rips on their hands. Rips are when your skin rips apart from wear and tear. Sometimes they bleed, sometimes they burn, but they are something most gymnasts will experience. In my entire gymnastics career, I only got one rip. I showed my coach and he was shocked. He said, "Oh my goodness! Everyone off bars!" I chuckled because it was a running joke. If Terin got a rip, we were over doing it. Many people ask me how I prevented rips. The only thing I can say is that although my sweating hands were a pain in the butt, in the end I think it saved my hands. Also, I wore tape grips every day, whether I needed them or not, to prevent wear and tear on my hands. When I went to the Olympics, I actually made 101 tape grips so that I could have one for every training session. I also had three pairs of grips ready to go at any time. I loved the tight feeling of new grips, and I switched grips every two weeks.

Every athlete goes through "burn out," or a phase where they want to quit. It's normal. In fact, I would say you are not normal if you have never experienced it. So what is it that keeps you going to the gym day in and day out? For me, it was regret. Why would I want to work my entire life and give up the last two years of high school? Sure, there were things I would rather be doing. I would like to go on vacation with my family, go on dates, go to parties, or even go to prom. But what if I quit? Would I be thinking about it for the rest of my life? Absolutely.

My dad often told me how he much he wished he would have stayed with sports in college. He regrets it to this day. I remember thinking that is so long to regret something in life. If I can stick with it for just a little longer it will all be worth it. I didn't want to go through life with regrets.

In any sport, there will be good days, there will be bad days, and there will be days you don't want to get out of bed. But if you do, if you push yourself towards your goals, you will never say, "I wish I would have." As my coach always said, "Coulda, woulda, shoulda."

Action Box:

Focus on your routine or project you have to get done. What is that project?

Create a timeline:

....

....

....

....

Create a to-do list:

....

....

....

....

Chapter 3

Turning Weakness into Strength

In gymnastics, an athlete will always have a weak area. My advice to you is turn that weak area into your strong point. Learn how to compete. Sounds simple, right?

I hated beam. I dreaded it every day. I was terrified to compete in it. Two years before the Olympics I must have fallen on damn near every beam routine I competed. My attitude was awful when it came to beam. I knew I had to change my outlook on this event or I wouldn't reach my ultimate goal of competing in the Olympics. So from there on out, I changed my attitude from "OMG, I have 10 beam routines" to "Wow, I only have 10 beam routines."

I made it a competition. Each time I stepped up to do a routine, I told myself that it's not just that I'm going to make a beam routine, it's how *good* am I going to make this routine. I mentally put myself in stressful pressure sets. My internal voice said,

"Okay, Terin, this turn will determine your future. This turn, the National Team Coordinator is watching."

As much as I hated my coaches stopping the entire gym to watch a pressured set, it was extremely helpful in the end. I wanted to feel that shaking your body feels when you are nervous competing because I wanted to learn how to control it. The year before the Olympics and from then on in my elite career, I never missed a beam routine. I became known as Terin, the rock and the consistent gymnast. I knew I could get up and hit a beam routine anytime and any day.

I was once asked how I changed my attitude. I will tell you, it doesn't happen overnight. It's really a reverse psychology strategy or fake it until you make it. When I found myself thinking negative thoughts about the beam, I quickly corrected myself. I was really big on visualization for each routine. To get better, though, instead of visualizing a perfect routine, I visualized a mistake. I know that sounds crazy, but visualizing the mistake helped me understand what to do to correct it. This way when I did the routine in real life, I didn't panic with every little mistake I made. Otherwise, forget about it – train wreck city.

Action Box:

Fake it Till You Make it!

Think about your biggest weakness – what can you do to improve it?

....

....

....

....

Why do you think this is your weakness? It is because people say it is, or are you telling yourself that?

....

....

....

....

Have you ever had a "fake it till you make it" moment? Describe it here.

....

....

....

....

How did you handle the pressure?

....

....

....

....

Chapter 4

My Best Failure

In 2003, I was picked to be on the World's team. It was something I had expected, but still, I took advantage of it. I knew I should be on that World team, and I never thought it could be taken away from me, so I became complacent. Once in Anaheim, California, I was training with the World team in the practice gym. In my mind, I was doing it to the best of my abilities, but I was fooling myself. I was saying that I was doing the best I could, but in reality, I wasn't. I wasn't reaching my full potential. I was simply going through the motions. I was just trying to hit a routine rather than hitting the *best* routine every single time.

Chellsie Memmel, a phenomenal athlete and friend whom I look up to even to this day, had competed at the Pan Am Championships and won a few days prior. The National Team Coordinator at that time decided Chelsie had a better chance than I did at winning a medal at Worlds because she was coming off a fresh win. As a result, I lost my position on that World team. Following the decision to take me off the team, I was forced to train in a different gym by myself with very bad equipment. It was such a big wake-up call for me. In the end, I was chosen as an alternate and was able to attend the games, but sitting in the stands watching the team train on the World podium on my 17th birthday was a pretty sucky birthday present.

At that very moment, I made a promise to myself. I would never give anyone else my spot from here on out. I wanted to show the Selection Committee how big a mistake they had made. Instead of crumbling when my spot was stripped from me, it ultimately became my biggest motivation. This particular experience was the best teacher of my life. My coaches fought for me to stay on the team and said I didn't deserve my spot being taken away, but if it hadn't been, I never would have trained harder, better, smarter. I wouldn't have become the athlete who reached her true potential.

There were some very unfortunate events that happened that year at Worlds. Courtney Kupets tore her Achilles tendon and Annia Hatch devastatingly tore her knee while training on vault. Ashley Postell ended up getting violently ill and had to go to the hospital. I was sad for my teammates. I knew how much they wanted the U.S. to win the gold. That's when I was asked to step in. The National Team Coordinator came and asked me to come off of alternate status and compete.

Of course, as an alternate, I hadn't had the chance to train or practice on the competition floor. In addition, there was not a 30-second touch for us. The touch is basically a warm-up period for athletes to get on the equipment before they compete in their next event. Because of the live television coverage at Worlds, they had taken away that opportunity. This meant that my first time on the equipment – competing for the second highest competition in gymnastics – I was competing without feeling out the equipment, as gymnasts say.

Talk about being a mental/emotional mess! I could not show anyone how nervous I was. I had to be tough. As my grandfather used to say, "This world's rough. You gotta be tough." On the inside, I was so nervous I wanted to run away and hide. On the outside, I was the most confident I could be. I knew I could go out and do the best I could because I had trained my whole life for a moment like this. I could not let the doubt of others or doubt of myself ruin this moment. An athlete can give up when it gets tough, or they can show the world, their teammates, their parents, and most importantly, themselves that this is what they work for in the gym day in and day out.

The USA only had five competitors at Worlds, one less than all the other countries. Still, we managed to go out, do our best, and win the first ever gold medal as a team!

The win was incredible, and it was also a release. We had so many trials, challenges, and struggles that it was overwhelming to realize we were still a team with so much talent. It was really emotional for all of us. We all stood on the podium, teary-eyed and filled with pride. With the bright spotlight on us, in our American flag leotards, we all fought back our tears. Through sickness and multiple injuries, we still managed to be on top of the world. It was so overwhelming, and we were all so happy.

There was a sense of accomplishment and pride that can only be felt when you achieve success by overcoming challenges. As the flags were raised for the top three countries, the American flag rose above them all. Our coaches were either screaming for joy or crying along with us. We were all just so proud of each other. I don't think America knew about all the struggles Team USA had overcome and how big a deal the win really was. Every team has ups and downs, and I think we were dealt the worst possible hand we could have been dealt. But we stepped up as a team, and we left there as an even stronger team.

Action Box:

Write down an example of a time you felt you had failed.

What did you do to overcome that failure?

....

....

....

....

How did it feel when you achieved success?

....

....

....

....

Chapter 5

Making the Olympic Team

From the time I was nine years old, my coaches began telling my parents that I would be going to the Olympics. But my dad is very realistic – he just wanted me to focus on getting a college scholarship. Because of that, I didn't start thinking seriously about the Olympics until I was 15 years old. At the time, I don't think I really understood what it meant. It's odd because even though I was an elite athlete, I still felt like I was in the middle. There always seemed to be more ways for me to challenge myself and keep improving. Each year, I worked my way up and made all the teams. Eventually, though, it became clear that the only one I had left to make was the Olympic team.

Once I began to think about it seriously, my mom and dad began to see the possibility too. At one point, I even made them promise that if I made the team, they would let me get an Olympic tattoo. As the reality that I could make the team became even more apparent, my parents realized they were going to need to quickly come up with some money to help me get there.

Fortunately, Bank Midwest and Applebee's agreed to sponsor my family, and they did it on really short notice as well.

Every four years, only four to six girls in the entire United States make the Olympic gymnastics team. The odds are nearly impossible. Many, many people told me and my family that I couldn't do it. At times, I believed them. But even if I couldn't make it, by God, I would at least die trying.

It's probably a good thing I'm stubborn, and I love to prove everyone wrong. I made the 2004 Olympic team, competed on the beam, and won an individual medal on the uneven bars. I even had a squat turn on the beam named after me. Oddly enough, I never placed on the uneven bars at any competition in my elite career except the Olympics. In fact, I actually competed at Level 5 for three years in a row because I wasn't good enough. Then all of a sudden, there I was, on national television when the Selection Committee made their decision on who would compete and represent the United States at the Olympic Games in Athens, Greece. It was the first and only live selection ever to be done with gymnastics. They called our names, one by one: Carly Patterson, Courtney McCool, Courtney Kupets, Terin Humphrey, Mohini Bhardwaj, and Annia Hatch.

I was completely overwhelmed when they called my name. I was in shock as tears ran down my cheeks. Hundreds of questions raced through my brain – did I just hear them right? Is this a mistake? Do they trust me enough for this? I remember thinking that maybe it was a mistake.

And then realizing it wasn't. I did it! I made it! I was in complete shock trying to get a grip on whether it was real. And then I suddenly realized the deal I made with my parents was going to happen, too. I was officially an Olympian from Bates City, Missouri, a town of fewer than 200 people. And I was finally going to have a tattoo of the Olympic Rings.

Action Box:

Have you ever wanted something so badly in life?

What is the timeline you've set for reaching this goal? A day? A week? A year? Five years?

....

....

....

....

And what is your strategy for achieving it?

....

....

....

....

How often do you put in the work to achieve your dream?

....

....

....

....

Chapter 6

Athens, Greece

There we were. After attending the Olympic Team Training Center in Houston, Texas for a few weeks, we were suddenly in Athens, Greece. We had arrived at the Olympic Games. It all seemed like a dream. By this time, I had been away from home for a month already, and I just wanted to indulge in a pizza. At the same time, I was ready to compete and get it over with.

The Olympic Rings were painted all over the streets and signs about the Olympics were everywhere we looked! The dining hall was unbelievable. I kept pinching myself to remind myself that it was all real. As I passed athletes I had seen on television, I was completely surprised because they were asking for my autograph. Some of the big names I had only seen on television such as Cătălina Ponor and Svetlana Khorkina were walking and training among us. It was so overwhelming, and I kept telling myself to get it together.

The opening ceremonies were the night before we competed, and it also happened to be my 18th birthday. Because the ceremonies lasted for so many hours and women's gymnastics were the first sport to compete, our team could not participate in the opening ceremonies. We couldn't risk our legs being sore. Instead we just rested and watched the opening ceremonies on the television that our vice president had purchased for our living room the night before. We spent the evening in our rooms watching "Saved by the Bell" episodes Courtney had on DVD. We iced and heated our bodies to get ready for the competition.

It's so hard to explain the Olympics, but I can tell you that they are tough. You spend your entire life training for this moment, and then in one minute and thirty seconds, it's over. There are no second chances. Millions of people are watching. You feel both excited and nervous, and yet you're ready to get it over with because you know the next chapter of your life is about to begin.

My family showed me support every step of the way. They sent me daily cards and daily inspirational quotes that I kept and put in a scrapbook. These quotes and daily inspirations helped me through one of the most difficult times of my life. There wasn't one day that I ever felt alone from my family, even when we couldn't see each other or speak on the phone. There were some mornings I cried because I wanted to spend my birthday with my family, but the love they showed me while I was away was priceless. I knew I was loved no matter the circumstances or outcome. I think that's important as a parent to just be there for your child during competitions. The stress is already through the roof, so just be there and show them love. In the end, I was there to do my job. I was there to be a soldier; I was sent out to be on the Olympic stage.

They say people who have "out of body experiences" are crazy. I'm here to tell you that I believe they are very real. It happened to me during the event finals. Svetlana Khorkina, my idol, finished competing on the uneven bars, and then it was my turn. As I started my routine, the strangest sensation came over me. I felt light, and it felt as if I was floating. It seemed like I was watching myself from above doing my bar routine. It was the strangest moment I've ever experienced in my life. Individually, it was one of the best routines I have ever done, and I ended up with an individual silver medal.

The Olympics were a bittersweet moment for the U.S. team. We were the reigning World Champions, and everyone expected us to win the gold medal at the Olympics. At the time, Russia and Romania were extremely dominant in this sport, but we were the fan favorites. Unfortunately, instead of the gold, we won silver. In some ways, we were disappointed. We had expected a different result, and we felt like we had let everyone, including ourselves, down by coming in second. However, it didn't take long before the realization sunk in that we were Olympic medalists. I mean, how many people win an Olympic medal?

Being on the podium with my team and having our flag raised above the other countries was a very humbling, honorable moment. It was a moment I can't put into words. The Olympics were a slightly different feeling for me compared to Worlds. It was hard to believe that I was an Olympic medalist. It was more of an individual journey of success. I felt like I had overcome obstacles that were thrown at me. I had been one of the biggest underdogs and I went on to become an Olympic medalist. I took my spot back and showed the world that I did indeed deserve to be in the Olympics. In fact, I didn't just deserve to be in the Olympics, I was good enough to win a medal. Nobody can ever take that away from me. But honestly, to me it wasn't about the medals. It was about the sacrifices my family and I had made. It was about the blood, sweat, tears, and pain I endured to reach my goal. I had accomplished one of the hardest things any human being can do. All of this hit me as I was standing on that podium and again, I cried. I cried because I was so overwhelmingly happy.

Action Box:

What are some of your individual accomplishments?

....

....

....

....

What could you have done better?

....

....

....

....

How did you feel at that moment?

....

....

....

....

Where you proud of yourself?

....

....

....

....

Did you ever think, "Wow, what's the next chapter in my life?"

....

....

....

....

Chapter 7

What Fame is Really Like

On my way home from the Olympics, I wrote down everything that I couldn't wait to eat. My food list covered three pages. The moment my mom picked me up from the plane, after my hometown teammates greeted us with posters, balloons, and the first initial media, we went straight to Taco Bell, Einstein Brothers, and Godfather's Pizza where I indulged for hours. Beyond that, the next few days were a blur. I did interviews at radio and television stations and attended school parades. I couldn't go to Wal-Mart without someone stopping for a picture or an autograph. I was a hometown celebrity and Missouri's most decorated gymnast.

We had to be packed and ready to go on a three-month tour in less than four days after our return from Athens. We didn't even attend closing ceremonies at the Olympics. We toured 48 cities in three months. I deferred from college for a semester so I could do the tour. We walked the red carpet at movie premiere events. We attended concerts and sports games. We were treated to every suite of every event we attended. Although this experience was great, it was also overwhelming. I was honored to feel like a "hero," but I wasn't equipped to handle what came with it. People who would never talk to me before suddenly tried to become close to me. People had ulterior motives and attempted to take advantage of me for the title.

This is a hard spot for most Olympians. They don't know how to adjust back to the normal life they lived before the fame. There is a sense of entitlement that comes with fame, but fortunately for me, my parents snapped me back really quickly. My mom still asked me to do things for her, and my dad would say, "Excuse me, you're how old? You can do it yourself." We lived on a farm and we had cows and horses. It didn't matter that I was an Olympic medalist, I still had to take care of them. It was hard juggling a normal routine with the media tour. At times, it was super stressful.

Many people want fame, but we don't always know what celebrities have to go through. One of those things is having to deal with stalkers. I have had two stalkers in my life. The first one happened when I was around 15 years old. This person knew every time my brother and my dad would leave town and when it was just mom and me alone. He would call on the home phone in the middle of the night. One night he called me and said my horse was going to die. It was really scary and unfortunately, the police couldn't do anything. The next morning, my mom and I woke up and went out back to find my horse had a cut so big on his leg and that he couldn't walk. It was infected, and he ended up dying. To this day I never knew who this person was or what had happened.

The other stalker I had was as an adult. This man showed up at my place of employment. I had no idea who was calling me over to talk. I asked him if I could help with something. He asked, "You don't recognize me?" I replied, "No, I don't. Do you have a child in gymnastics?" He laughed and said we had met at a party one night in college (which was in a different state many years ago), and I had been really nice to him. He said he needed to speak to me outside in his car. I quickly said no and turned around and left. This man left the building but stayed in the parking lot until a man in the gym went out to confront him. Then he took off. I was able to get his license number and called the police. His license plate came back not on file.

As this was unfolding, I remembered I had received multiple messages from three separate Facebook accounts. After that day I received around ten hate messages from the three separate accounts with three separate names. Then one day the messages just stopped. I had an agent look him up from all the miscellaneous names I knew and found out that he had been deported back to France for violating probation.

Action Box:

It's important to enjoy your favorite treats or meals once in a while. What are your favorite "cheat" meals and treats?

....

....

....

....

When you feel overwhelmed, what do you do to slow your brain down or relax?

....

....

....

....

Chapter 8

College

One week before I went to Alabama on a full ride scholarship, I remember sitting in my room crying. I didn't want to do gymnastics anymore. I wanted to be normal. I wanted to be fat and go to parties. I wanted to date. I just wanted to be a normal teenager.

Besides that, I also wasn't sure if my body could handle it. Coming off the tour, I really had two choices: I could go pro and make money from endorsements, or I could earn a college scholarship. At the time, social media wasn't a thing, though, so athletes who were doing endorsements didn't make the kind of money that athletes make nowadays. In the end, my family and I didn't believe I would make enough money to be able to go pro, so I accepted a scholarship to the University of Alabama.

It wasn't long after coming off the tour that I was back on the road making the 12-hour drive to Tuscaloosa, Alabama. As I entered the University of Alabama campus, I stopped at a red light. Looking up, I couldn't believe it. It was me – only me – on a huge billboard advertising Alabama gymnastics. The pressure hit me like a ton of bricks. I suddenly realized that this city was counting on me.

If anyone asks me about my collegiate experience, I say the same thing. I had the best time of my life. I don't regret it, and I found myself and grew up in Tuscaloosa.

But if you read what's on the internet, you will learn that I let everyone down by *only* winning two individual bar titles. Maybe I did, but I also overcame more obstacles than most. I had some demons I was facing. One of those was the toxic relationship I was in. I experienced emotional, physical, and sexual abuse. There were times that I came into practice with bruises on my arms. I did my best to cover them with makeup, but it didn't always work.

On top of that, my body broke down. I was just physically done. I loved this sport so much, but after years of high impact and intensity, my body was having no more. I had two double elbow surgeries, three nerve blocks and two blood patches in my back. It was my back that ultimately ended my gymnastics career. My last day of practice, just a day after three epidural shots in my back, I was doing my bar routine. As I went into my toe hand, it felt like ten knives went through my back. It paralyzed me and I was stunned. I couldn't feel my legs and couldn't walk, so I crawled to the locker room.

I remember thinking, "I can't do this anymore. I want to be able to walk. I want to have a family. If I keep this up, my body won't be able to handle being normal." I called my mom that day and told her I couldn't do gymnastics anymore.

The next day, I came into practice and the media was there. I thought that was odd. One of the reporters approached me saying, "Congrats on your retirement!" I was stunned. I hadn't spoken to my coaches about this. Then I was told that the coaches made the announcement earlier that morning. The emotions I felt were overwhelming. I was shocked and stunned. They were correct. I was done. But I would have liked to have a warning.

Leaving my senior year was a roller coaster of trying to cope without gymnastics and learning what it meant to be "normal" like I'd always wanted. On top of that, I didn't leave gymnastics on a high note. Rather, it was one of the lowest points in my life. My coach wanted me to stay and at least support the team my last year, but I just couldn't walk into a gym. I was so burned out from the sport; I hated it. I also struggled with personal relationships with my teammates. I do not blame anyone. It was a difficult time for me, and so it was my fault as well. But I definitely struggled with some of the girls. It all meant that I wanted to be as far away from my teammates and the sport as I could.

To try something different, I decided to intern at a law office. It was such a blast and I learned so much. I spent my last half a year working and getting physically healthy, but emotionally I was struggling. I struggled with finding myself. I had always been "Terin the gymnast," and now I wasn't sure who I was without gymnastics. I also struggled with an extremely toxic relationship. After one very big physical incident, I called my dad. When I heard his voice on the other end of the line, I couldn't speak. I just sat there on the phone, and he sat there quietly with me. Eventually, I told him that I needed to come home. I didn't tell him what happened, but I said that I had to get out of that town. A week later, after graduation, my dad came and got me and brought me home.

Action Box:

Have you ever been stuck in a situation you just didn't know how to get out of?

How did you handle it?

....

....

....

....

Who was there to support you?

....

....

....

....

Chapter 9

Life Now

I read somewhere that over 75% of Olympians go into depression after the Olympics. They get stuck in the stardom phase, which is short-lived. It's only a matter of time before the next generation of athletes comes up and takes your place and you are forgotten. So Olympians are left with, "What now? What do you do when you have reached and accomplished your biggest goal in your life, that one you worked for years to achieve?" Those were the same questions I was asking myself. So what now?

After college, I moved home. I had no idea what I wanted to do with my life. I always loved forensic shows, so I attempted to work in a ballistics forensic lab. I absolutely hated it. Staring into a microscope all day was extremely boring. I needed more, and I still didn't know what I wanted to do.

The next thing I did was move back to the Kansas City area and started coaching, but I still needed more in my life. My brother suggested that I sign up for the police academy. I chuckled. How was a five-foot, 100-pound female going to make a difference as a police officer? He kept encouraging me to just try it. So I did; I enrolled in the police academy. Once again, I found a purpose and started working out and training for it.

One cold January morning in 2010, I was in line during a training session wearing blue sweatpants and our police academy T-shirt. Looking around, I was very nervous that everyone was going to laugh at me. Without warning, I heard the first boom from a blank shotgun round. Here we go! Doughnuts were being thrown at me, and Lord have mercy, it was exciting. Several of my classmates were in tears, shaking from the drill. Fortunately, my brother had given me the best advice and told me to just never act intimidated.

So there I was, thinking this wasn't too bad while people around me were ready to quit. Then they moved us to the gym area. Hundreds of police academy alumni and police officers were yelling and screaming at us. It was loud and very overwhelming. At one point, I looked over and realized they were yelling at me in a good way: "Go, baby Humphrey!" I quickly learned that's what I got for attending the same school as my brother.

From that point on, though, it was a breeze. I found something I was good at, and I broke all of the girls' records. I almost beat the push up record as well, coming in second behind only one other person, my big brother. Yes, I went through the tazing and macing like most officers do. I was also the first one hired out of my class, and for the first time since the Olympics, I felt like I had a purpose.

For four-and-a-half years, I was a police officer, and I will always be thankful for the time I spent in that career. It was a very humbling, eye-opening experience. I loved it and I wouldn't change my experiences for the world. Being a police officer taught me to always document everything, no matter whom you feel like you can trust. This skill came in handy later down the road when I was an Athlete Representative.

As a police officer, I'm a survivor. There were so many life-or-death situations that I experienced during that time, including almost being crushed by a spinning car. There were also gut-wrenching situations, like the time I dragged elderly patients from a senior citizen home that was on fire. People in the crowd were spitting on me and telling me to leave them there to die.

Another time, I sat with a family who found out that their six-month old baby had just suffocated. I survived many crazy situations, and I am definitely a better person because of it. After four-and-a-half years, though, I was forced to choose between the two loves of my life – gymnastics or the police force. Although I had seriously considered becoming a detective, the department I was in didn't have much room for promotion, so I ended up choosing gymnastics. In the long run, I still wonder if that was the best decision.

Action Box:

Have you ever had two options in life, such as two separate jobs offered to you at one time?

How did you make a decision?

....

....

....

....

Did you write out a pros and cons list?

....

....

....

....

Did you confide in your parents or significant other to decide?

....

....

....

....

How did that impact your life?

....

....

....

....

Chapter 10

Athlete Representative

In 2009, I was approached by USA Gymnastics and asked to run for the Athlete Representative job. This meant I would be one of three people who would vote to choose the World and Olympic teams. I was honored. Unfortunately, when I ran for the position, I did not win. I fell short to Nastia Liukin.

Someone once told me, "Terin, the athletes would be very lucky to have you as their representative, and I think you are here for a reason." I took that to heart, and so even though I remained a police officer, I took time off without pay to stay involved in gymnastics and to better myself by going to meetings for the athletes. There were times where I would work my normal 12-hour night shift, get on the plane in the morning, and work all afternoon and evening for gymnastics. It was a lot to bear, especially when I was only volunteering.

In 2012, Nastia resigned as the Athlete Representative to train for her comeback, and that's when I stepped in as the main representative. This was such a difficult role. I went from

controlling my own destiny as a competitor to deciding someone else's destiny. Although it was an honor, it was devastating
to watch the athletes work so hard and fall short. As an athlete
myself, I knew how difficult it was to qualify, and watching the
ones who didn't make it was heartbreaking.

Although I had an alternate rep, she was rarely in the picture, so I ended up wearing many hats. I tried to level it out by
keeping my role on the selection committee a priority and keeping my relationships professional. Then once the competitions
were over, I relaxed a little more and was able to eat dinner with
the athletes and hang out with them afterwards. I held meetings
with the athletes and asked them to speak up if any concerns
were present, and I did everything I could to make them feel at
home.

On some occasions, I was part of the medical personnel. I
held limbs for athletes whose arms were dislocated. I took care
of them and sat with them in hospitals for hours when they had
concussions. I was their support because their families could
not be there. I would do it again in a heartbeat. Most of the athletes were very kind and appreciative and even came back to
thank and support me to this day. They knew I did what I could
for them. I don't regret being there, physically and emotionally,
for them during their time of need.

However, others were not so appreciative. This often
shocked me, because the athletes were so talented and so fortunate, and I don't know that they fully understood how great

they had it. I struggled with their actions and the sense of entitlement that some of them felt. Don't get me wrong, I would do it again, but it wasn't easy. In the end, I was left with the confirmation of my belief that coaches and athletes should be held to a higher standard and that they should act accordingly.

Action Box:

Have you ever tried the best you could at something with the best of intentions, but still felt taken advantage of?

Would you do it over again knowing in your heart that you did the best you could with every opportunity given?

....

....

....

....

Have you ever had a friend, a teammate, a classmate, anyone that has ever come back years later to thank you for something you did?

....

....

....

....

If so, how did that make you feel?

....

....

....

....

Example: I had an athlete who messaged me telling me how thankful she was for me being there when her parents couldn't be at the training camps. I started crying because I was so stunned at her appreciation and it overwhelmingly made me so happy it put me in tears.

Chapter 11

The Tour

I don't want to seem dramatic, but the 2016 tour was one of the most challenging experiences of my life. I was a chaperone for the kids under 18 years of age. It was like being the babysitter nobody wants while you are at a party for months. One of the dangers of being a celebrated athlete is that there can be a sense of entitlement. Just because you're an Olympic or high-performance athlete doesn't mean your values need to change or that you have to forget who you are.

I have been in situations where athletes assume they can brush off their bad behavior because of their celebrity status, and I am certainly not above this either. What I have learned is that you just want to be able to sleep at night. Yes, you can go and have the time of your life, but at the same time, it's important to remember your actions may come back to haunt you.

During the tour, my grandfather died. I had to fly home and attend to my family. Being away from my family for 63 days was hard, but enduring a tragedy while I was gone was very rough.

After I returned back to tour after the funeral, I only received one condolence even though there were over 20 athletes. I think most were just happy the babysitter was gone.

Then at the end of the tour, with only three days left on tour, my grandmother suffered a massive stroke. I told the person in charge I needed to go home early and be with my family. I was told if I went home, I would not receive my compensation. After giving this organization 10 years of my adulthood and my entire childhood, I was denied compensation. I stated that I would be flying home and I would fly back to finish the last day of the tour. At that time, I needed the compensation to keep my house.

Fortunately, I did end up coming back and they paid me. But once again, I was reminded that even though the spotlight can shine on the talent and achievement of great athletes, there is much more to the story.

Action Box:

Have you ever done something that made you feel disappointed in yourself?

People aren't always perfect and on top of their game. We all make mistakes and are human, but what is something you do that you're really proud of?

....

....

....

....

"Americans always love a good comeback."

– Unknown

Chapter 12

Gut Feelings

I'm often asked whether I knew the infamous Larry Nassar. In short, yes, I did. He was our team doctor in the 2000s. However, I only visited Larry Nassar one time during my time as an athlete. His treatment did not help my particular injury, and I was fortunate to never need a doctor. I've always had the mentality of not trusting anyone at first, and secretly, they need to gain my trust.

That was very true with Larry Nassar. I never liked him and just felt the creeps around him. Luckily, he wasn't around me often. As an adult, I've often wondered if my "creeps" were real. There were very few encounters with Larry. In fact, he went to the ranch (the National Team's Training facility in Texas) approximately two times a year. I did sit in the training room with the girls on a few occasions but was asked to leave due to HIPAA laws. I also was told by coaches that my place was not in the training room because I was on the selection committee and they were uncomfortable with someone on the selection committee knowing their athlete's injuries. Then I was told by athletes that they would like their alone time without any adults, and they were bonding with their teammates.

This tragedy still haunts me, though. What Larry Nassar did is nobody's fault but his own, but what he did was tragic, and in my opinion, it destroyed the gymnastics world for a few years. When something so awful happens, people often look for someone to blame. People in positions of power were blamed because perhaps they knew about his past and let him stay anyway. Others, like me, were blamed for not speaking up when, in fact, we didn't know. Some blamed me for not being supportive of the athletes, and it was hard to take the criticism. I quit my job for those girls and did everything I could to help them. I simply did not know anything more, and nobody can act on the "creeps." In addition, if the victims couldn't tell their own mothers or coaches, why would they tell me, someone they didn't see nearly as often or have as close of a relationship with?

In the end of my Athlete Representative experience, I was trashed on social media. Social media gave people a forum to voice their opinions without facts. In May of 2019, five months short of my maxed-out term of being an Athlete Representative, I was asked to deal with an athlete who was bullying other athletes. I spoke to the coach about her behavior, and to my knowledge, it was dealt with. After that, I posted a meme of Nick Saban on Facebook. He is the Alabama head football coach and I have been a huge fan of his since I grew up in Alabama.

In the post, I stated, "I would be the first to admit I needed a good butt chewing growing up." My point was a reflection on my own experience as a person who was once a lazy athlete and was able to become the hardest working athlete. A cowardly L.A. attorney took my meme and twisted it. I could not sit back and let this man bully me. I was not raised this way, so I called my mom and told her that I had to do something. I knew this situation would affect my parents just as much as me. Both of my parents agreed with me, and I had their support. In my heart, I knew I needed to face him versus hiding from him. I reacted to his response and publicly fired back.

The following Friday, I spoke to the CEO. On Sunday morning, she sent two people to come and ask me to resign. The CEO followed up with an email stating that she had spoken to their attorney and head of the board, and it was in their best interest for me to be gone. Being on the inside of an organization that you want to believe is a good organization, you hope they have your back. Yet after giving USAG my childhood, a medal for our country, and ten years of my adulthood, they let me down. I asked them numerous times to take me off the internet. They refused. I asked them not to post this incident on the internet. They refused. In the end, they publicly fired me.

Following that, the cyberbullying began. People posted things that would surprise you. I even received death threats. It caused me, my family, and my unborn child to deal with more stress than most people do in a lifetime. Being fired is one thing, but being fired publicly while pregnant is another. I couldn't believe it. I was stunned.

At one point, the stress became so overwhelming that it resulted in a really strange incident. Walking out of the grocery store after doing my shopping one day, I suddenly stopped. I was so confused. I had no idea where I was or who I was. I had no memory. The only thought I had was, "Where is my dog?" I walked up and down every row of the parking lot until I found my car. Then I called my mother and told her I didn't know what was happening. I made it home, but the anxiety and stress were overwhelming. I didn't make it to work for an entire week. Fortunately, I had a great support system and was able to take care of myself until I felt better, but the stress definitely took its toll.

Although I don't feel the entire situation was handled well by USAG, I am a stronger person today because of my experiences. I handled everything to the best of my ability, and if it meant saying goodbye to USAG, then that's what I needed to do. Larry Nassar is in prison today because of his actions, but so many innocent people were affected, including me.

I want to be clear. I want athletes to share their experiences – the good, the bad, every part of it. I encourage everyone to tell the truth so they can move forward. Kids today deserve to have a good experience. They deserve the money, and everyone deserves to move on and find peace.

I'm thankful for my experiences as the Athlete Representative, but I'm sad that this has ruined my name in the sport that I worked so hard at for many, many years. I'm sad for the pain I endured and the pain my family has endured. I'm sad that people define gymnastics as Larry Nassar. I'm sad to the past athletes who had to endure the abuse alone. I believe that USAG failed them, and they failed me as well.

Action Box:

**Have you ever had a gut feeling about something
or someone and it turned out to be true?**

What did you do about it?

....

....

....

....

How did you feel after? Guilty? Shocked?

....

....

....

....

Chapter 13

Cyberbullying

Cyberbullying is on the rise. As sad as this is, cowards say things behind the computer rather than to your face. Suicide rates are rising very quickly because of cyberbullying. Why are people stooping so low and acting like children, throwing fits because they have a different opinion from another? The first time I was cyberbullied, I let it get to me. I was depressed and developed paranoia. From then on, I was scared of doing something for fear of being put on the internet. I don't understand why people are so quick to form an opinion about something they know absolutely nothing about.

America, we can do better. I encourage you to go back and erase or refrain from future posts you may not have all the facts about. I will be the first to admit, I let the trolls get to me and control my life. I'm here today to say "not anymore." Never again will I allow myself to fall victim to someone who has to put others down in order to feel better about themselves. The bullying, degrading, belittling, and name-calling has got to stop.

For the longest time, I was told by USA Gymnastics to keep quiet. Don't do interviews. Don't speak out about anything! I wanted my voice back, and I am here to say I no longer care what this entity says. I'm no longer a prisoner. My plan is to speak out, speak out, and speak out some more. USAG failed to protect *us* athletes. They failed and are failing to protect the coaches. They failed to protect me. Even now, they are continuing to fail.

And so here I am again, wondering what to do with my life after USAG. I'm left with "what now?" What do I do with my life? I need more.

Again, I have hit rock bottom. I see my friends getting college coaching jobs, and I wonder whether I should be further along with my life. I don't have all the answers, but I do know that the situation with USAG left me with opportunities. It pushed me to move on with my life, and I can pursue other careers if I so choose to. Terin Humphrey has experienced pain, but Terin Humphrey is not a victim. No matter what I have gone through, I will not be labeled a victim. It is my choice to move on and I will not play the blame game. Do I believe some attorneys and some people in power need to be held accountable? Absolutely. But I believe in karma, and I believe the man upstairs will always settle the score.

This is not a book to ask you to feel sorry for me or point fingers. I know people make mistakes, relationships grow, and sometimes both parties are at fault. At the end of the day, I think the experience has made me a better person, and I will focus on that going forward.

Action Box:

What are your thoughts about cyberbullying?

....

....

....

....

Is there anything you can do to combat this epidemic?

....

....

....

....

Chapter 14

Here's My Advice

I am always asked what kind of advice I would give to aspiring Olympians or girls wanting to be police officers in a male dominated world. It's a road less traveled. Here's what I will say:

1. Make goals! Make lots and lots of goals – daily, weekly, monthly, and long-term goals. Originally, my goal was not to make the Olympic team, but rather to get a college scholarship. At 15 years old, I knew I had to change my goal. I needed more out of gymnastics because my potential was the Olympics.

2. Follow your heart. You know yourself better than anyone. If you are miserable, change it. Sounds simple, right? Sometimes it's not, but better to move forward rather than stay stuck in the same spot.

3. Save money. This may be difficult, but this goal has helped me tremendously. When you feel lost in this world, you may need to take it easy for a while, and it will be important to

have some backup means to help you until you find what you are supposed to be doing.

4. Family always comes first. Your family are the only ones who will stick by you through thick and thin without ulterior motives, and they have your best interest at heart. My family has picked me up more times than I can count. My family picked me up when I was physically beaten in a toxic relationship, threatened with a gun, and when my house was broken into by an ex-boyfriend. They drove two hours to pick me up at 1:00 a.m. when I wasn't answering my phone all day. I will never be able to thank them enough.

5. Slow down! We have one life to live. Enjoy it!

6. Trust your intuition.

7. Eat the food!

8. Be organized.

9. Learn something new every day!

10. Have grit. Have tough skin.

11. Other people don't define your self-worth. Your accomplishments can't be taken away from you.

12. Don't feel guilty for overreacting. You learn from your feelings. If that's how you felt, then own it.

13. Don't spend your time worrying about things that haven't happened (I struggle with this one). Most of the time,

things never end up happening and we waste that time stressed, worried, and anxious.

14. It's OK to be selfish. Take care of yourself. Take long, hot baths, go on peaceful walks, lay out by the pool, go shopping for *yourself*, take that vacation, and get massages. As women, we tend to everyone else's needs and often forget about our own.

15. Don't rely on anyone but yourself. You are in control of your situation, your money, and your life. It's never too late to fix that.

16. Small steps – if it's just to get out of bed for the day, get out of bed the most graceful way and make that bed!

17. Failure is inevitable. It's how you get back up after the failures that matter. When you lose yourself; keep your eyes open; sometimes your biggest opportunities come after your biggest failures.

18. You are beautiful without makeup. Remember, most of your idols are photoshopped when you see them on the Internet, TV, or in magazines. Don't be fake! You don't need fake hair or fake boobs. Smiling is the best medicine and the best accessory.

19. Take care of your teeth!

20. Never listen to negative people because they will always have something to say. Even at my best, I had people saying

on the internet I was ugly. My knees were knobby. My eye shadow was too sparkly. My boyfriend is ugly. Who cares? I was not put in this world to make others happy.

21. Keep positive people around who you love and make you happy. I have found that people love to watch people fail. Why? As women, let's stop this!

22. A grudge is a heavy thing to carry for the rest of your life.

23. Respect yourself enough to walk away. Don't be taken advantage of and don't settle.

24. You are not alone in this world. Don't be afraid to ask for help.

25. Everyone has a purpose in this life. What's yours? Live your life like it's your last day on this earth. Life is what you make it. Find *your* passion – not your parents', not your friends', *yours*. Also, as women, sometimes we lose sight and our self-worth in a man. Do not miss an opportunity because of a man unless he is there to stay.

26. Life is hard. It's challenging. And some days are a struggle just to get by, but excuses don't get you anywhere.

27. Never cheat, in sports or in life. It gets you nowhere. Hard work beats talent any day of the week.

28. Take a leap of faith when you are scared.

29. If you fall, get back up! Don't stay down for long. Take a personal day and get back up!

30. Do what you love to do. Your heart is a powerful tool to make you successful. Follow it.

31. Being honest and truthful doesn't win you many friends, but it will win you the right ones. There were two girls who stood up and stood by my side at school. You guys know who you are. You are amazing friends and I'm proud to still call you both friends!

32. Failing is the first attempt at learning. Most importantly, never give up. You owe it to yourself to become successful. I read once that if you are born poor, it is not your fault, but if you die poor, it is your fault. I love this saying because it's not about money. Being rich can mean being rich on life.

33. Forgiveness shows strength. Forgive them even when they are not sorry. If you carry bitterness throughout your life, who is really winning? They are.

34. Live on your own and learn how to make it on your own.

35. It's human nature to chase power and money. Don't chase power. Chase happiness.

36. Be careful what friends you choose. They may be around for years, but may not always have your best interests at heart.

37. Appreciate your parents. I won the silver, but my parents won the gold!

I have experienced many ups and downs, many failures, much success, and a lot of heartbreak. But I do not have any regrets. I've had the highest honor of serving my country by competing in the highest possible sporting event and won two medals! I've served and protected as a police officer for four-and-a-half years, and I've served and given back to future athletes as best as I could. And as you can see, I have learned so much in the process.

Here are a few of my favorite quotes:

"Happiest girls are the prettiest girls."

– Audrey Hepburn

"This world's rough. You gotta be tough."

– Harold Willis

"Sooner or later, everyone sits down to a banquet of consequences."

– Robert Louis Stevenson

Action Box:

What are some of your favorite quotes?

....

....

....

....

....

....

....

....

....

....

....

....

....

....

....

....

Keep these quotes somewhere that you can see them every day so they continue to inspire you to take one more step toward your ultimate goal(s).

Chapter 15

What's Next?

My goal was to get my story out and write a book, so I will cross this one off my list. However, it has taken some courage on my part. Speaking out about my own experience of domestic violence is very hard. My experiences with USAG were also very hard. In this book, I have shared my story, and maybe in sharing it, I can help someone else.

I have never had a dream in fashion designing or anything with "fashion" in it, but I was approached by a very caring and sweet lady named Noele Figueroa after my release from USAG. She is the owner and CEO of HIGO Apparel. She insisted I help her with leotards. I thought about this, and I thought maybe this could be fun! So one day I got blank sheets of paper and started drawing leotard designs. I felt as if this would be a great goal while I was pregnant. It required nothing physical, but I could still be working.

In September of 2019, Noele and I released "The Terin Humphrey Collection" of leos on HIGOApparel.com. My dream is to have my leotard line launch even bigger each year. Yes, a lot of the big names sell leotard lines, but I am in no way going to compare my leotards with any other line. Noele and I want to have fun while getting our collection out. 2020 will be our first test with this new dream of mine. We plan to attend competitions and run a leotard booth for young, aspiring athletes around the U.S.

I would love to be in a country music video. I grew up as the country girl and love country music. I always thought it would be fun to just be a part of a video. I am definitely not a singer, but to be in the video as the "model" would be cool. I know this one is weird, but it would be pretty fun.

I would love if my life story became a movie one day. The experiences I have had are a lot more than the average person. My career paths are a lot different and I think people would be interested in seeing my life on the big screen if ever given the opportunity.

I would love to learn how to speak and become a cyberbully advocate. This subject is very important to me, and I think so many people can relate to being a cyberbully victim.

I would love to continue coaching gymnastics and be the head SEC gymnastics coach at the University of Alabama.

I would love to be the director at the official Olympic Training site for gymnastics in Kansas City (my mom and I located it) under a solid entity. I know USAG is still pursuing this training site.

The FBI has always been in my mind. It was basically the only test I ever passed! However, this goal may not ultimately be a part of my plan. Part of the stipulation of the FBI is moving somewhere unknown, and I do not want to be away from my family.

Motherhood: starting January 2020 I will have my first child, a baby girl. There are so many emotions with this next challenge. I will be in charge of a little human being. I'm nervous, excited, and scared, yet ready.

One of my goals is to put out workout videos after my pregnancy for normal people who hate to work out but want to bounce back to normal.

I'm contemplating putting out a book dedicated to stepmothers.

Often people ask me if I will put my own children in gymnastics. My answer is that I am not sure. Although my journey was a success and I wouldn't change it for the world, I want them to make that decision on their own. Being an accomplished athlete is an honor that so few people experience, and I will be forever grateful for the experience and opportunity that gymnastics gave me. However, it came at a cost, and it isn't for me to decide the price my child will want to pay. That will be up to her.

Action Box:

What are your goals?

....

....

....

....

....

....

Often times, goals are more attainable if you say them out loud or write them down. If you keep them hidden, how are you going to accomplish them?

It takes courage to say your dreams or goals out loud. I encourage you to be a mentor and ask your little sister, your teammate, your classmate, anyone, what their goals are. Remember, some may be weird, and you will look at them as if to ask where it came from. But it's not up to you if it's attainable or not, it's up to you to be supportive and help them every step of the way.

And it's the same for you. Confide in your parents or your best friend and make your goals attainable.

Chapter 16

Final Thoughts

I hope you enjoyed my book and my journey. If you take one thing from this book, I hope it is to be kind. Stop judging people when only half the facts are given. Be on your own time and nobody else's time with life.

We all expect life to go one way, and it's not going to be like that. It doesn't mean that if you are derailed from your original plan, the next plan is better or worse, it just means it will be different than you expect. When life throws you curveballs, keep going. Keep fighting. Believe in yourself. Stand up for yourself. Be your best you, no matter what, and never forget who you are and where you come from.

Sometimes you will feel like you're in the middle – in the middle of jobs, in the middle of relationships, in the middle of drama. Sometimes you're walking on that thin ledge and you're not sure there is a safety net down below. That's life. When you feel that way, remember this – *never* give up.

Acknowledgements

My father, Steve Humphrey, who taught me integrity above anything. People can hate and be nasty to you, but you can't let them take your pride and integrity from you. Work hard the first time around so you will have no regrets throughout your life.

My mother, Lisa Humphrey, who taught me love has no limits. She is my rock, my main supporter, and the one telling me to get back on that horse and ride after I have been knocked off.

My brother, Shannon Humphrey, who taught me it's OK that people think a certain way about you. People will always talk about you and that's OK. What's not OK is you dwelling on their opinions. He is an amazing person and an even better big brother who always picks me up (literally and figuratively) when I fall.

My coaches, Al Fong and Armine Barutyan-Fong, who taught me to be the best gymnast I could be, but most importantly, a better human being. I will forever be grateful to them because they took a chance on a small town country girl with big dreams. They continue to be my second set of parents and mentors.

My former boss, John T. Sutton, an attorney who took a chance on me while I was struggling through life. He gave me a job and experiences that molded my law enforcement career. He always did and continues to make time for my stupid, silly questions.

Martha Karolyi, the former National Team Coordinator, who taught me that my best is never good enough. I have to push myself every day, every turn, and every second. Every turn counts.

Dale Carter, our local country radio station host in Kansas City. He believed in me before the Olympics when no other radio station did. He continues to follow my journey through this life and is so generous if I ever need a ticket or two.

All of the gym owners who allow me to coach their athletes during summer camps and allow me to sell my leotards during competition season. They allow me to spread my love, my knowledge, and my passion for this sport each year: Dan Alch, Sheila Bath, Sandy Flores, Al Fong, Joe Rapp, Cliff Parks, Lelila Burkett, Bryon Hough and many others.

People I would love to meet:

Bruce Willis. Colin Farrell. Angelina Jolie. Joseph Gordon-Levitt. Julia Roberts. Will Farrell. Jennifer Aniston. Vince Vaughn. Leonardo DiCaprio.

Favorite colors: Yellow and mint green

Sign: August 14, 1986 Leo

Action Box:

If you could meet anyone, who would it be?

....

....

....

....

Why?

....

....

....

....

Would it be someone who inspires you or just someone to make you laugh?

....

....

....

....

What would you ask them if you could meet them?

....

....

....

....

What advice would you give your younger self?

....

....

....

....

If you could go back and change anything about your life, what would it be?

....

....

....

....

Grab some paper, a calendar, and make your dreams come true. Remember, you have to start somewhere!

....

....

....

....

Terin Humphrey's Accomplishments

- 2003 Hall of Fame Inductee (first ever women's team to win gold at Worlds in Anaheim, California)
- 2004 Individual Hall of Fame Inductee
- 2004 Olympics in Athens, Greece
  - ➤ Silver Medal, Team
  - ➤ Silver Medal, Uneven bars
  - ➤ Humphrey skill named (squat turn 2.5) on balance beam
- Attended University of Alabama 2005-2008
- Two-time NCAA Bar Champion
- 2016 Missouri's Hall of Fame Inductee
- Missouri's most decorated gymnast
- Eleven-time All-American

- Graduated with a major in Criminal Justice and a minor in Psychology

- Worked in Ballistic Forensics

- Raymore Police Officer for 4.5 years

- Participated in American Ninja Warrior Seasons 7 and 8

- USA Gymnastics Alternate Athlete Representative from 2009 to 2012

- USA Gymnastics Main Athlete Representative from 2012-2019

- X-Treme Gymnastics Coach 2014-present

- Coached first Junior Olympic All-Around and Bar Champion in 2018

Made in the USA
Middletown, DE
11 January 2020